From My Grandmother's Heart

J.S. Roppolo

ALL RIGHTS RESERVED

No part of this book may be reproduced or transmitted in any form or by any means, electronic or mechanical, including photocopying, recording, or by any information storage and retrieval system, without permission in writing from the author, except in the case of brief quotations embodied in reviews.

Copyright Jonathan Roppolo 2018

All rights reserved

ISBN 13: 978-1732590533

ISBN 10: 1732590532

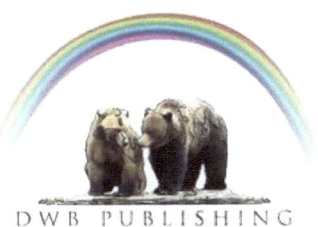

DWB PUBLISHING

Almost every child gives their grandparents superhuman powers. They're always the bravest and smartest people to ever walk the earth. Though it shows undying love and admiration from the grandchild, it's almost cliché.

But for me, it was true. Whether is was protecting her home from wild animals or taking time to tell me stories, I believed my grandmother was the smartest and bravest soul I knew. That, with her belief and compassion for others has served as an inspiration for me.

Recently, I came upon a collection of her poems, filled with her passion and wisdom. It's my hope that my labor of love in honoring her will assist you in finding the support and inspiration that you need.

Jonathan Roppolo

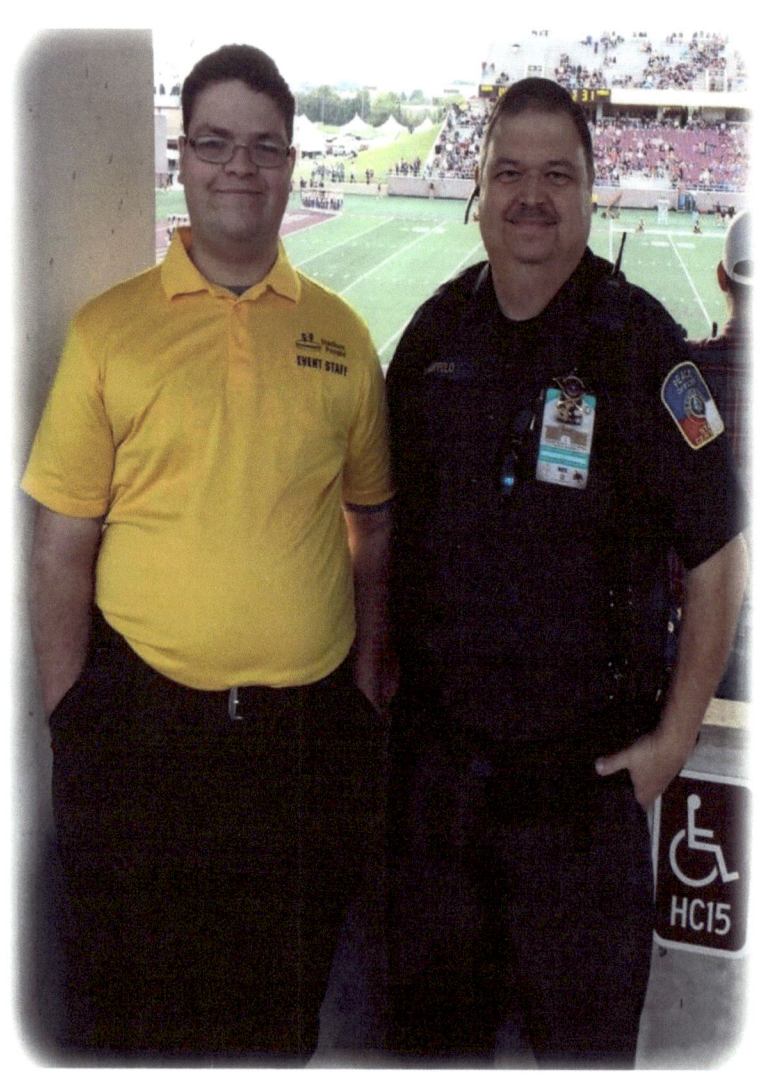

Our Keepers of the Peace

Across this land of ours
we have lawmen far and wide.
City, county, state and federal,
working side by side.

There should be cooperation,
dependability is a must.
They need to know that in a crisis
on each other they can trust.

Lawmen have a common enemy,
they share a common goal.
The stress wears on each of them
and often takes its toll.

But they don't need constant fighting,
each thinking that they rank higher.
They get it from the enemy...
there's no need for "friendly fire".

And so you fellow officers,
when on a friend you turn,
remember that someday
for their backup you will yearn.

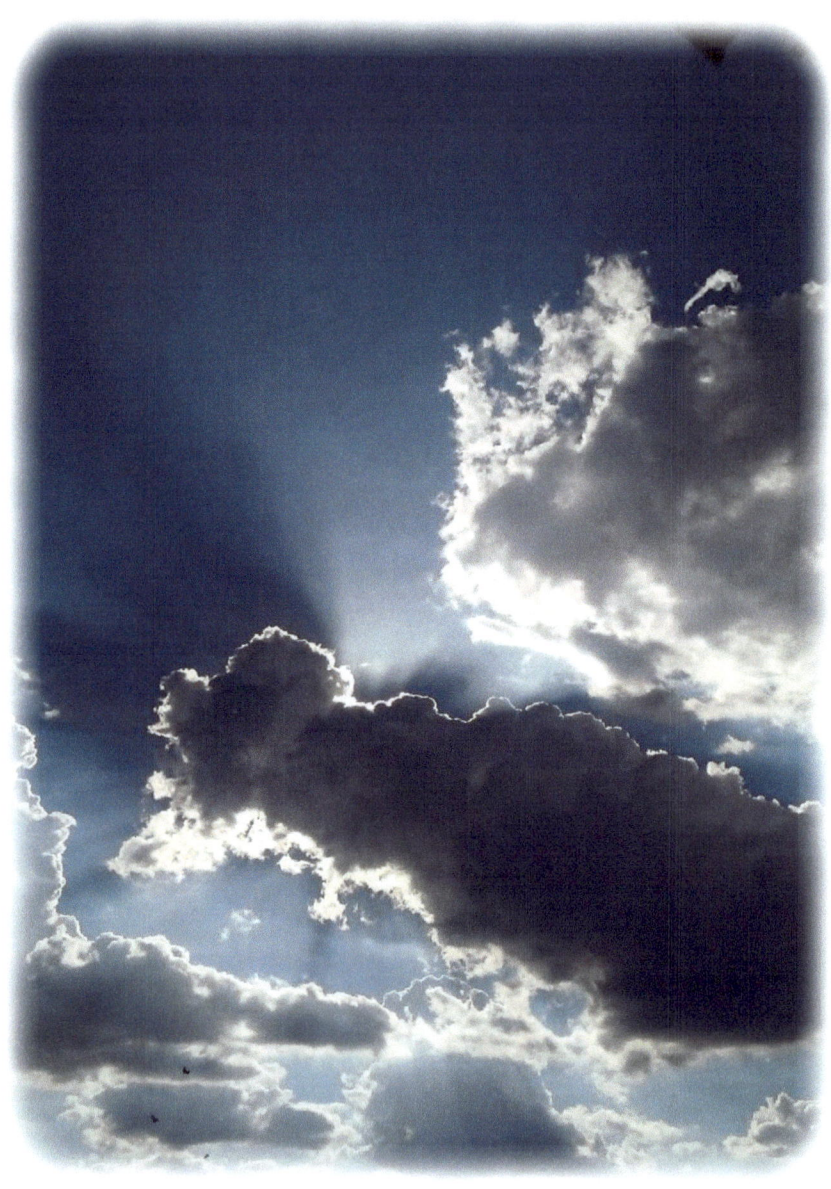

He Touched Me

He touched my life one summer day
my precious Savior so dear.
He spoke to me in quiet words
and told me not to fear.

The sin that held my life in chains,
invisible...but oh so real.
He came and gently took away
and His peace and joy I could feel

He turned my life around that day
as I asked him into my heart.
He gave new purpose to my life
that never will depart.

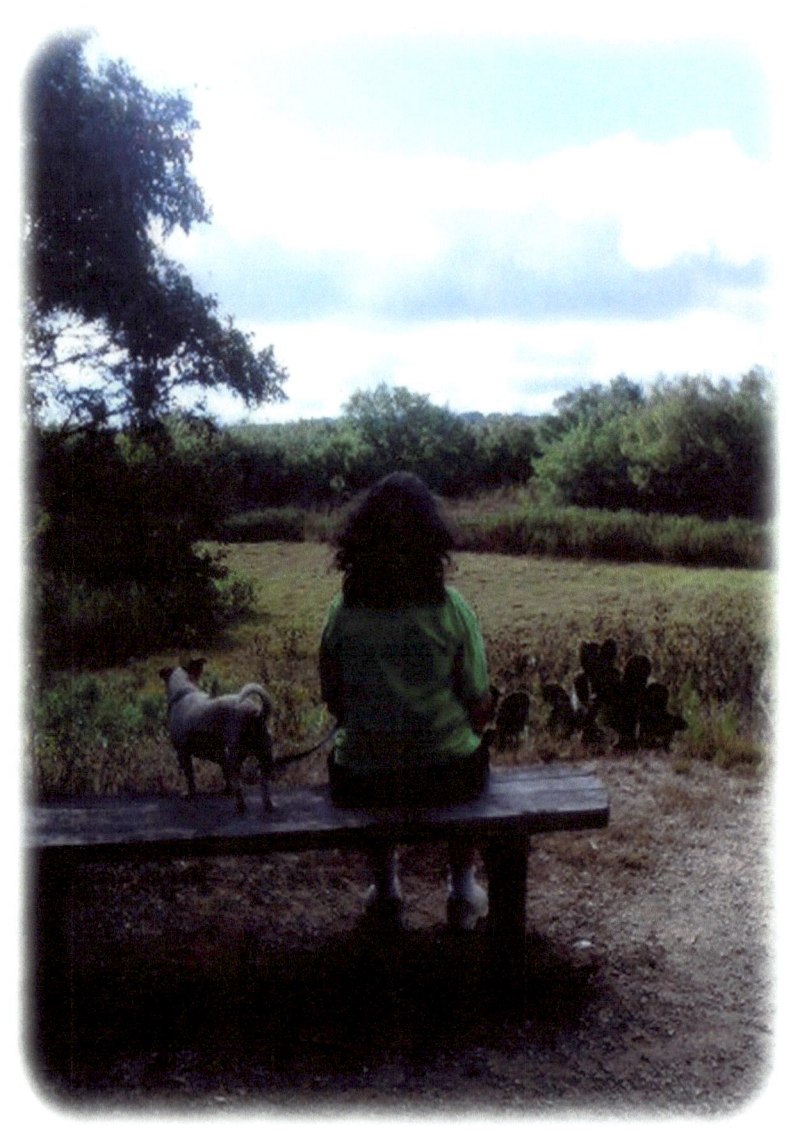

How About it Christians?

Have you talked to God today?
Have you told Him how you feel?
Did you thank Him for the morning?
Will you seek His blessed will?

He created the world in which we live,
made and put us on it too.
Will you show your love and thanks to Him
by everything you do?

Have you talked to Him about others,
those not yet within His will?
Did you go and witness to them
that the love of God is real.

My dear Christian friend,
as on this earth we trod,
we know that this is not our home,
and some day we'll be with God.

So as you travel day-by-day
be aware of His great love
and strive to help some troubled soul
find peace from God above.

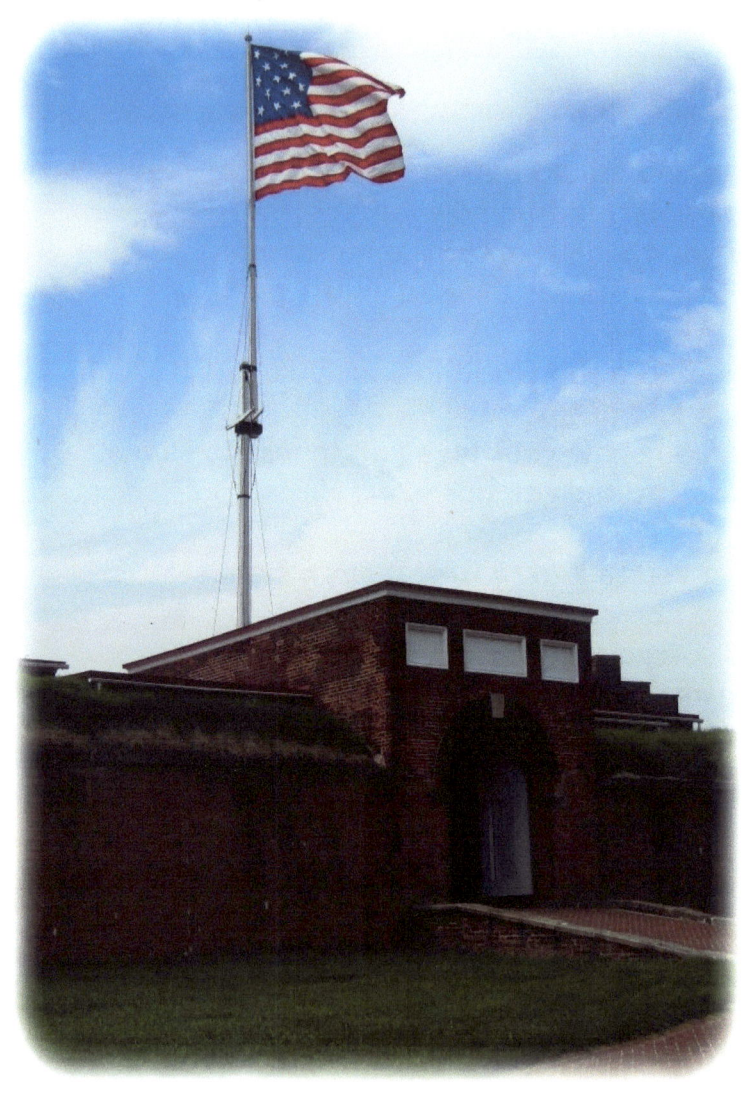

Fort McHenry

Baltimore, Maryland

A Tribute to the Soldiers

Editors note: This was written during the time of Desert Storm.

I watch as you leave your home,
family and friends.
and journey into a foreign land
where the desert never ends.

I watch your family as you go
their tears of sorrow mixed
with ones of pride.
I wonder at this ability,
their fears to completely hide.

As the days pass slowly by,
the war of worlds goes on.
Don't ever for a moment think
you are forgotten here at home.

I think about you every day
and as I talk to God
I pray that He will keep you safe
upon that foreign sod.

I pray the war will soon be over
and how happy we will be
as you then begin your journey home
and the Middle East be free.

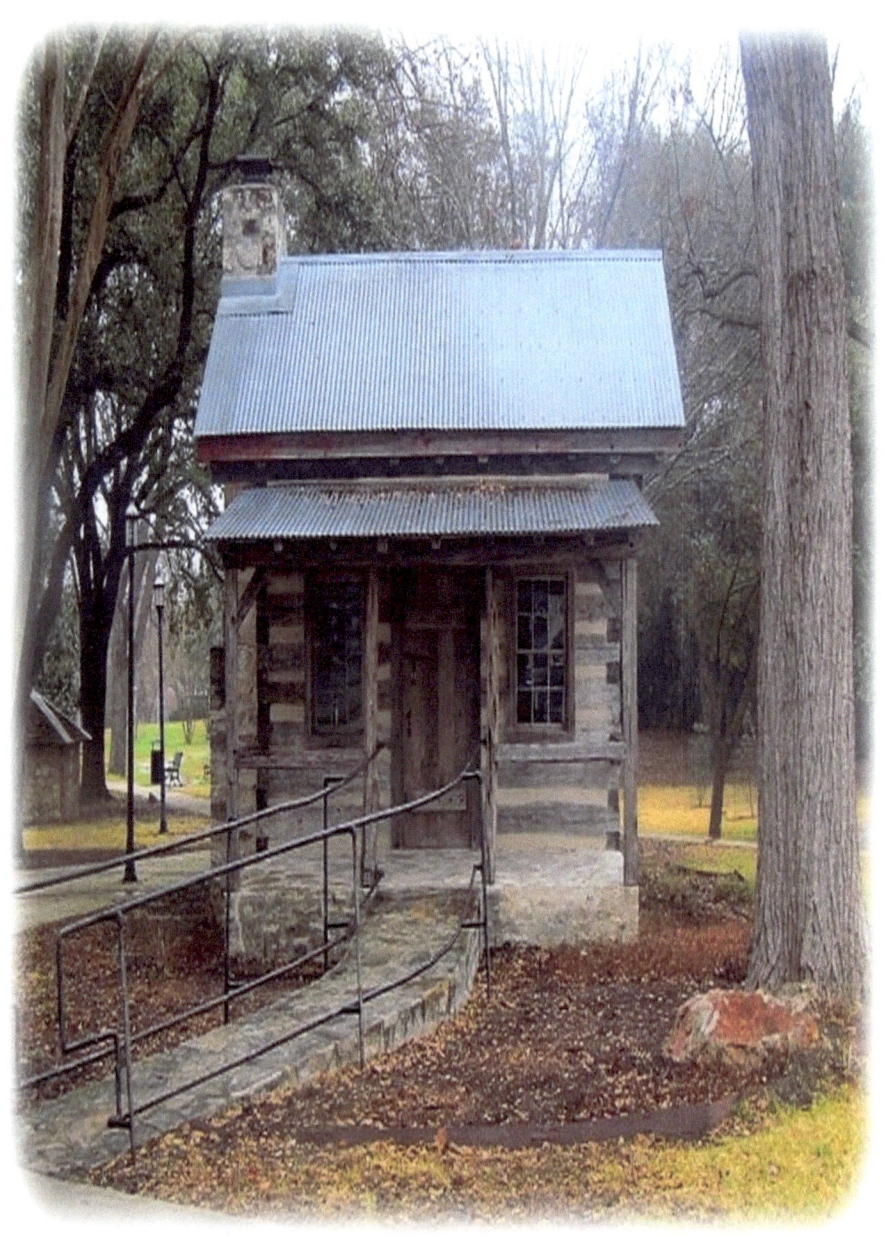

The Home's Foundation

I look back across the pages of time
and the days of my childhood I see.
My brother, Mother, Daddy and I
make up my family.

As all children must, we grew through
the years and left our childhood home.
With the loved one we had found,
we started a home of our own.

I thank God for my mother and my dad
who loved me and showed me God's plan.
They taught by example the foundation
of the home is the work of God...not man.

So I pass on to my daughter, the same
lesson I've learned to be true.
Trust God, not man, as you plan your
home.
He will not fail and will always be there for
you.

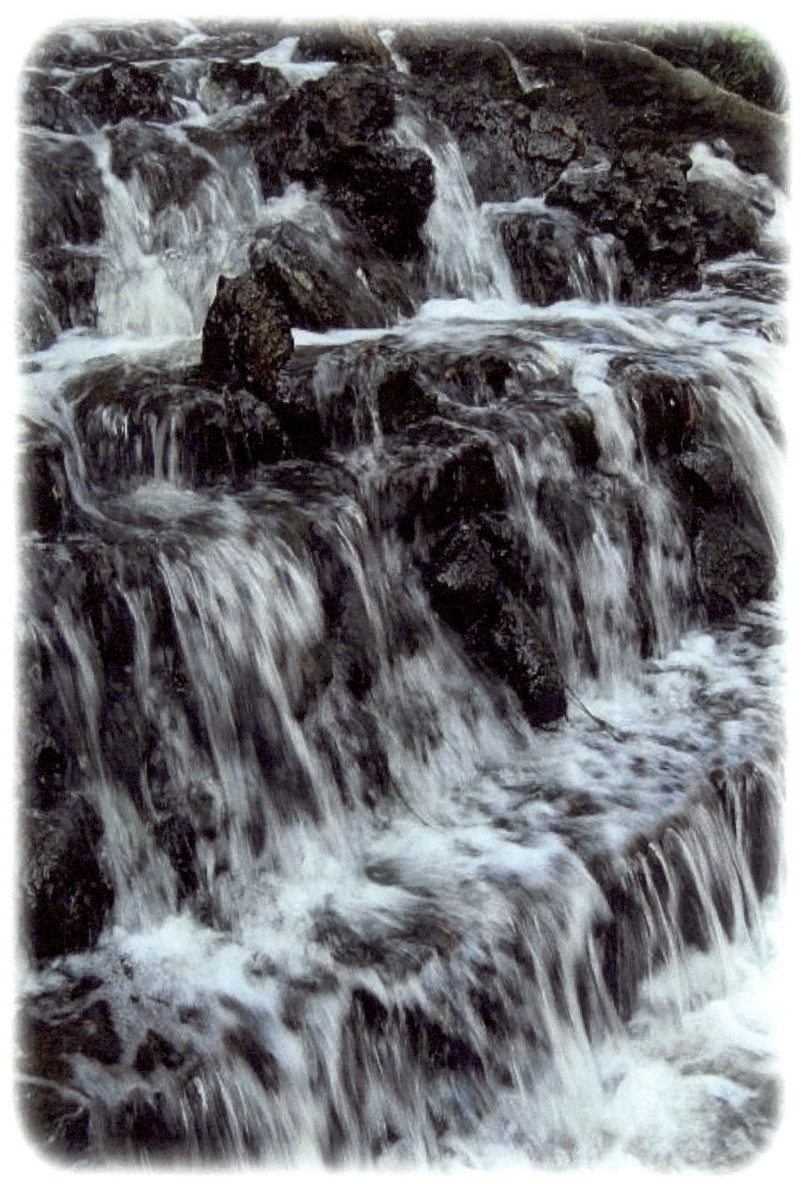

Let's Be About Our Father's Work

I read it in the papers and watch
it on TV.
It's the constant fighting of Christians
and it really bothers me.

God called us out as "special" ...
to go and spread His word.
How can we be used by Him
when strife is all that's heard?

Let us come before His presence
with a true and repenting heart—
with love for one another and
desire to do our part.

Let's be about the Father's work
till Life's race on earth is run.
And hear Him gently say
"Welcome home my child, well done."

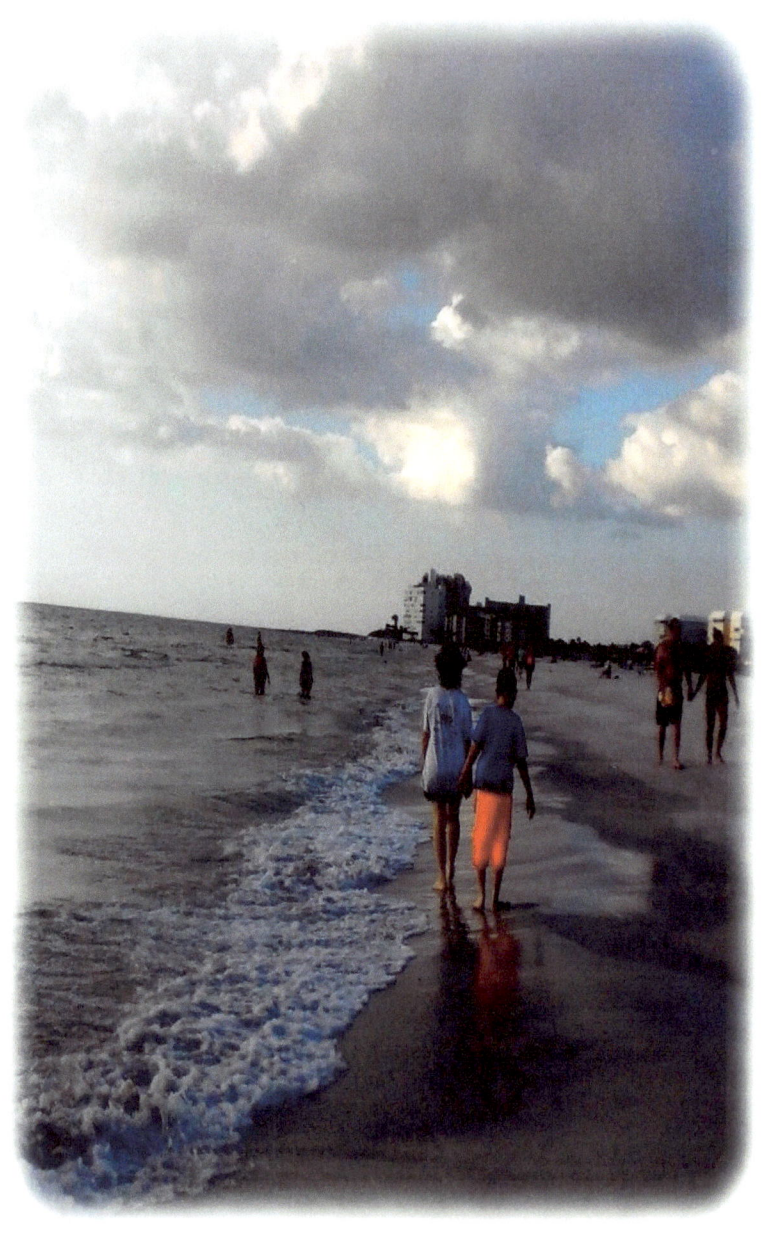

Teach Them of God's Love

The world is full of souls today
crying out in deep despair.
As we go about our lives, do we
see that they are there?

Are we sensitive to their dark plight
as through the world they roam?
Do we ever stop to give them hope
of an eternal home?

God saved us who believed in Him
and gave us this command:
"Go into the world and teach
that God loves every man."

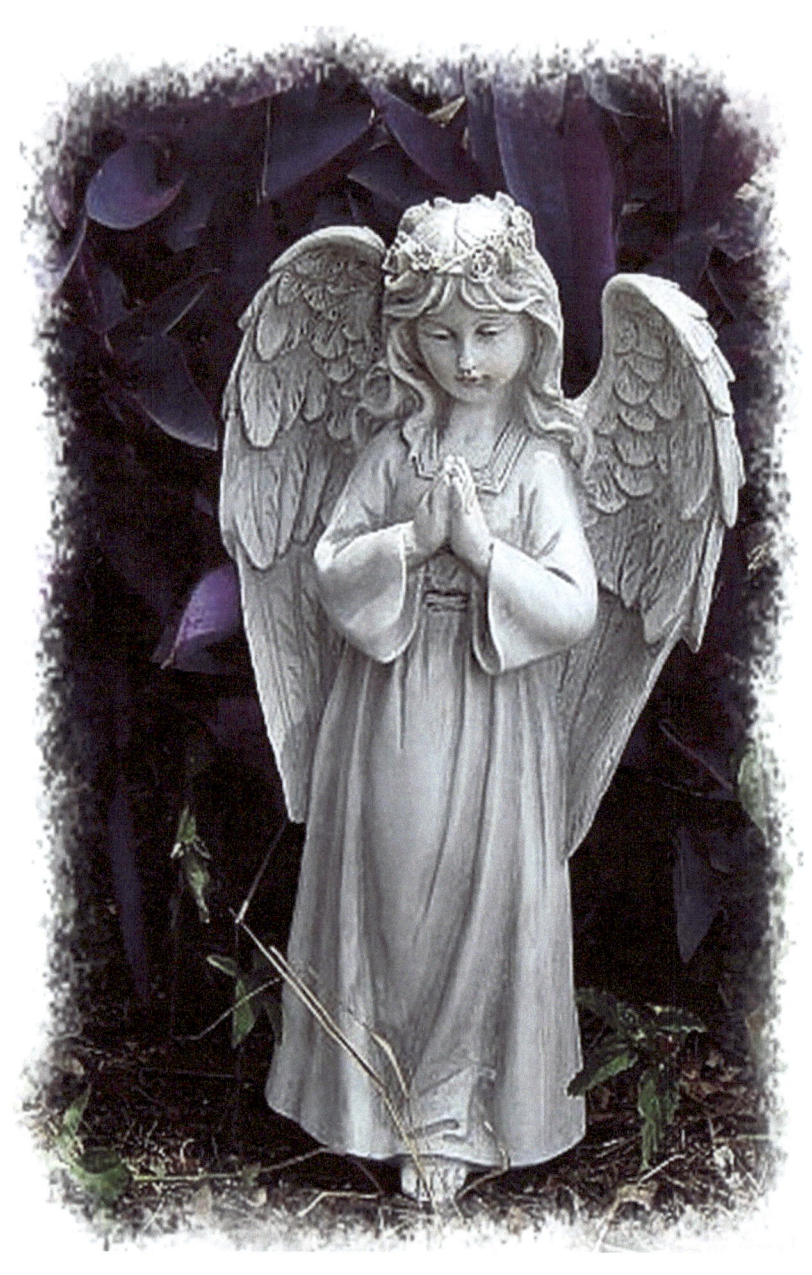

Mary, the Mother of Jesus

Long ago to the town of Nazareth
the angel Gabriel came, to a
young girl named Mary, and God's
will he did proclaim.

"You have found favor with God,
He has a special mission for you—to
be the mother of the blessed Jesus
is the service He would have you do."

Astonishment and trouble filled her heart.
How could these things be?
She had no husband, though betrothed,
God's plan she could not see

Gabriel told her "God would move"
and a miracle perform.
The Child would be His son,
there was no reason for alarm.

I am thankful she yielded her life to God
"Let it be as you have spoken."
So Jesus was born in Bethlehem
and the power of sin was broken.

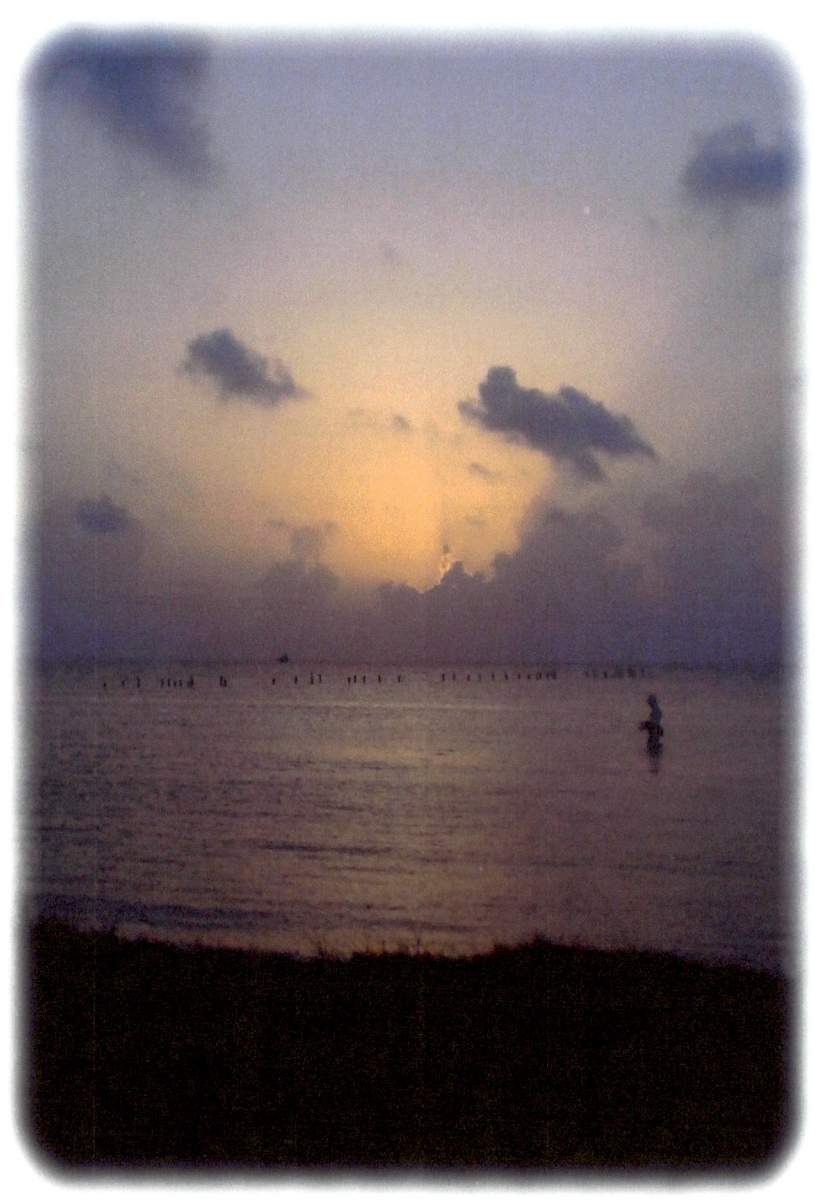

What Will You do With Jesus?

"What will you do with Jesus?"
Ponticious Pilot asked that day.
The angry crowd cried "crucify"
and they quickly took him away.

On a lonely hill called Golgatha,
they nailed Him to a cruel tree.
He gave His life for sinners.
Yes, He dies for you and me.

"What will you do with Jesus?"
The same question is asked today.
Will you open your heart and let Him in?
Or sadly send Him away?

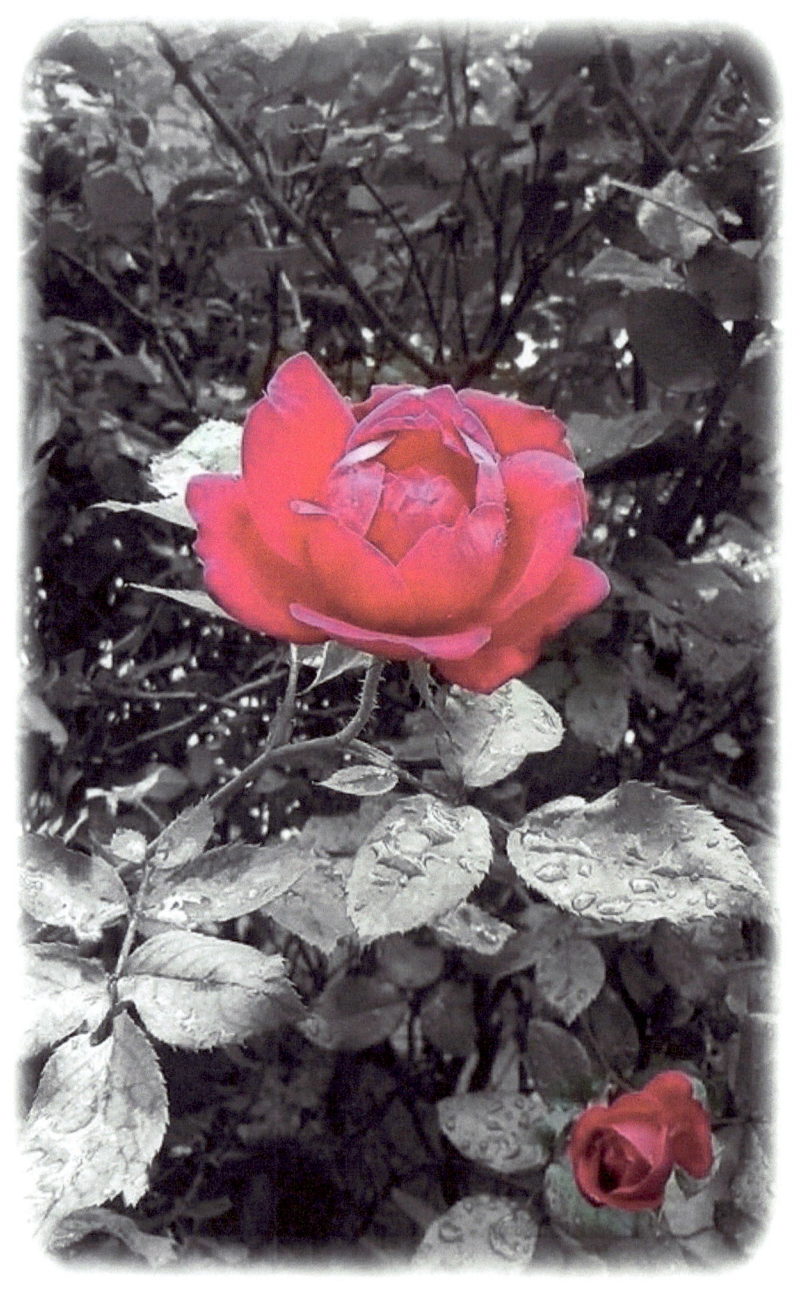

I Asked the Lord

I asked the lord to remove the pain
that plagued me so many years.
But instead He gave me strength to endure
and reminded me He was near.

I asked the Lord to remove my sorrow when
my loved on was taken from me.
He gave me peace and the will to go on.
His power and love was with me.

I asked the Lord strength for today
so the tasks I had be done.
He gave me power that came from Him
from morning till setting sun.

I do not know what lies ahead
as on this earth I trod.
But I know from whence cometh my strength;
my strength comes from God.

He'll give me strength to stand the test
when things aren't going my way.
He's willing and ready to help you, friend.
Just kneel to Him and pray.

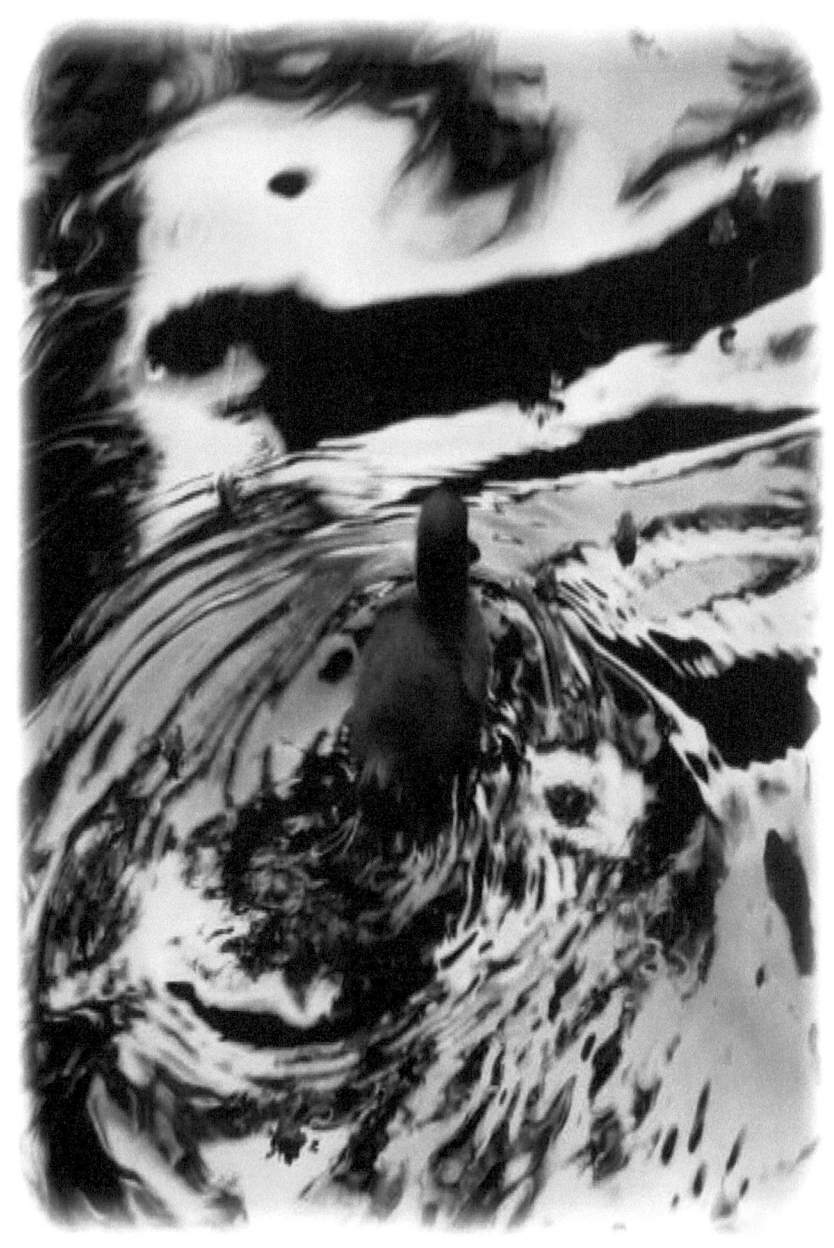

Now You are Twenty

So now you're twenty years of age.
My, the years have flown.
Yesterday you were my baby,
and now sweetheart, you're grown.

I wonder as I now reflect
upon those passing years.
if I was the kind of mother
who helped you face your fears.

Did I show you by example the
Christian way to live?
Was I always there for you,
and love and comfort give?

Forgive me if I failed you.
God knows I did try.
I love you now and forever.
My love will never die.

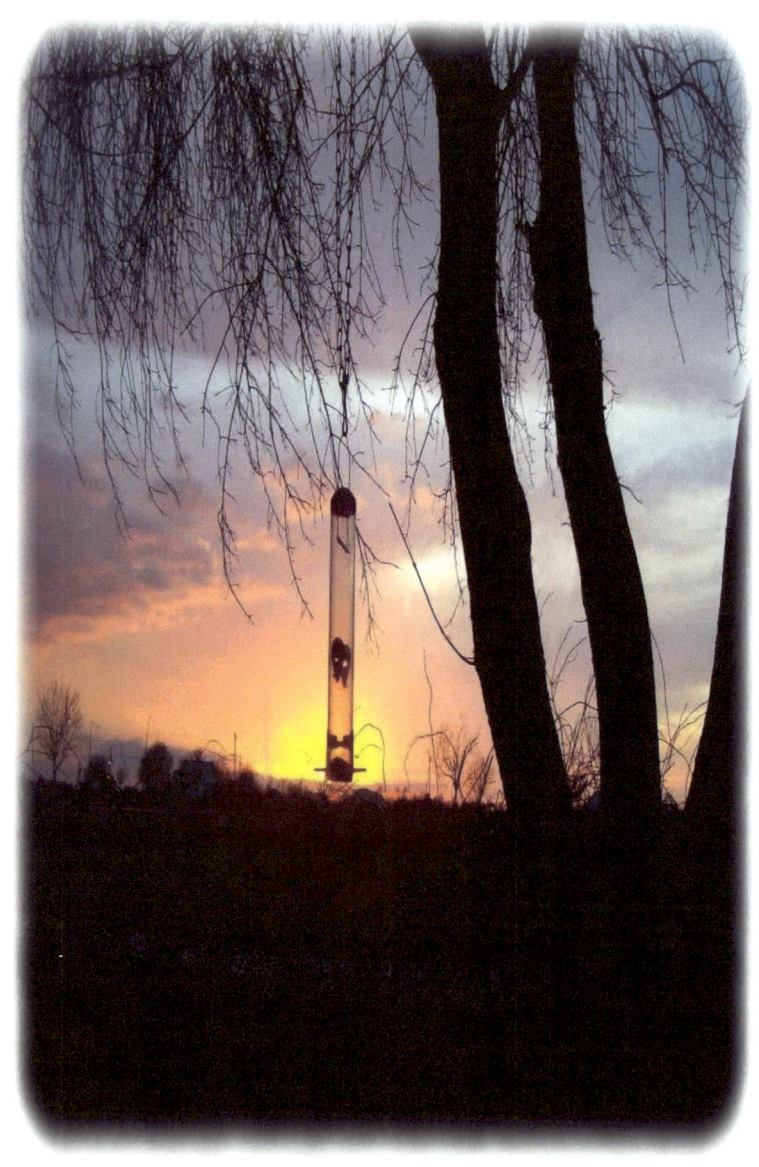

The Seasons of Our Love

In the springtime of our lives,
sweetheart, we joined our
hearts as one.
We labored side-by-side as Life's
race we did run.
There was trials, joy and heartache, as
all couples in life know.
But together we faced each test,
And on through life did go.

In the summer of our lives it seemed
our joys had been fulfilled—into our
home a baby girl one day came to live.
We loved, laughed, and cried together
as we fondly watched her grow.
Our lives had been made complete—
oh, we loved her so.

But into our lives one summer day,
the hand of Death reached in and
dealt a blow so very hard, it seemed
our lives would end.
Yours did end, my darling, and
quickly you were gone.
So sad the living then became—so
lonely was our home.

But in that future God has planned
for those who are His own,
we'll once again stroll hand-in-hand
in our eternal home.

And so good-bye in life I say,
sleep peacefully dear love.
I'll meet you on that shore one day,
In God's great home above.

About the author

Jonathan Roppolo is an award-winning photographer on a mission. Rather than judge a person or object on their physical appearances, he chooses to find the inner beauty. His photography reflects that.

Roppolo is an advocate for special needs people and is a member of several community-based non-profit organizations. He resides in the Texas Hill Country with his family.

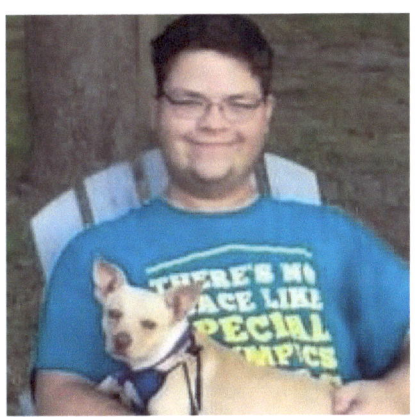

www.ingramcontent.com/pod-product-compliance
Lightning Source LLC
Chambersburg PA
CBHW040301220526
45473CB00002B/554